Part 1

Student
Activity
Book 1

PEARSON

Scott
Foresman

scottforesman.com

Editorial Offices: Glenview, Illinois • Parsippany, New Jersey • New York, New York
Sales Offices: Boston, Massachusetts • Duluth, Georgia • Glenview, Illinois
Coppell, Texas • Sacramento, California • Mesa, Arizona

ISBN: 0-328-26050-9

11 V001 15 14 13 12 11

Table of Contents

Name _____

Writer's Warm-Up

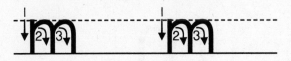

Name _____

Letter Cross-Out

Name _____

Writer's Warm-Up

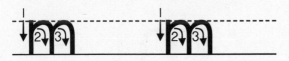

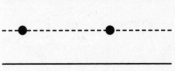

Letter Cross-Out

8

Name _____

Writer's Warm-Up

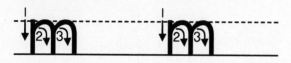

Activity 4

9

First Sounds

Name _____

Writer's Warm-Up

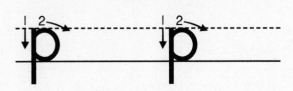

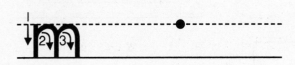

Name _____

First Sounds

p

_____

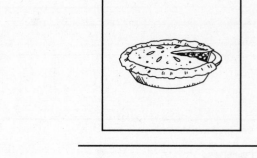

_____

_____

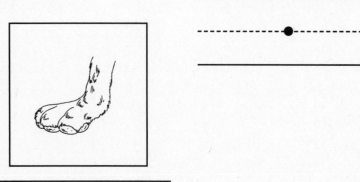

_____

_____

Activity 7

Writer's Warm-Up

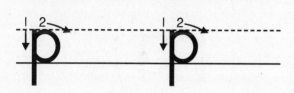

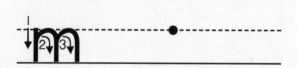 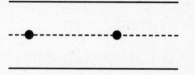

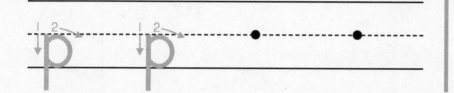

Letter Cross-Out

p m m

p p m p

m m p

p

Activity 7

14

Writer's Warm-Up

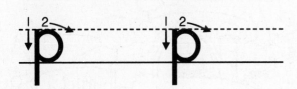

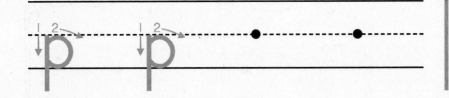

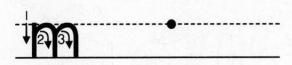

Letter Race

m

Finish Line

p

Finish Line

Writer's Warm-Up

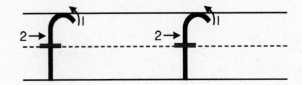

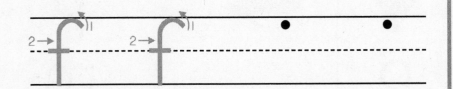
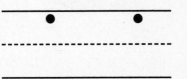

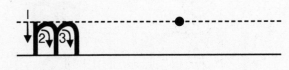

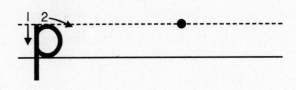

Letter Tag

→ m
♥
p

→ 🍎
p
m

→ p
★
m

→ m
p
🍎

→ p
m
★

→ 🍎
m
p

Name _____

Writer's Warm-Up

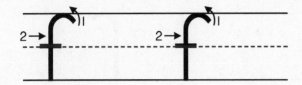

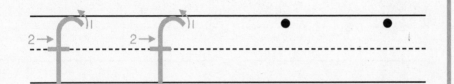 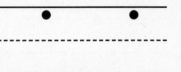

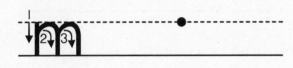

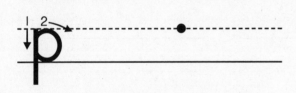

Letter Writing Game

m

p

f

Activity 7

Letter Mission

Writer's Warm-Up

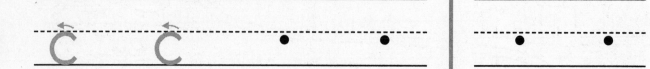

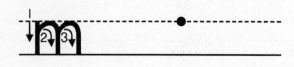

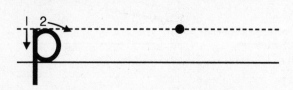

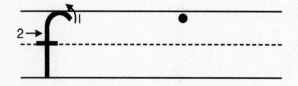

Activity 5

22

Name _____

Writer's Warm-Up

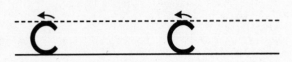

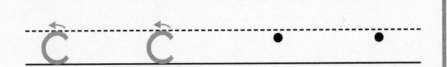 

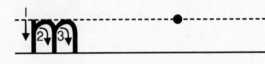

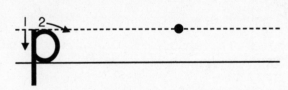

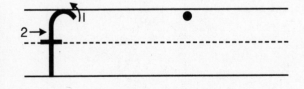

First Sounds

m p f c

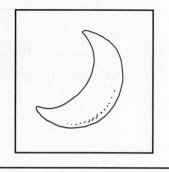

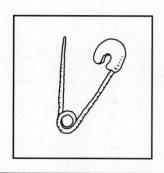

Name _____

Letter Cross-Out

f   c   m

p   f   p

m   f   c   c

f

Writer's Warm-Up

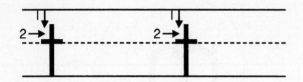

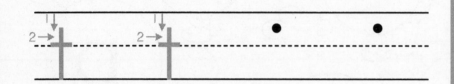

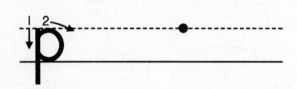

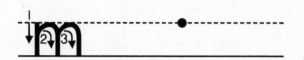

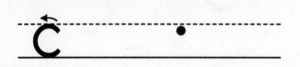

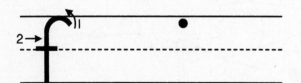

Name _____

Letter Race

Name _____

Writer's Warm-Up

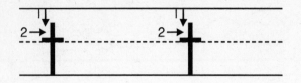

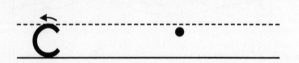

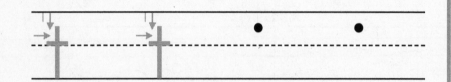

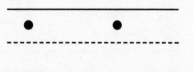

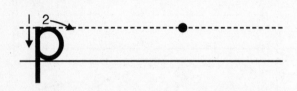

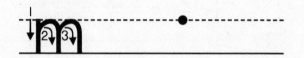

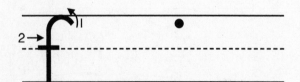

Name _____

Letter Tag

→ t c f

→ p f c

→ c t p

→ p m c

→ t c m

→ f p m

Activity 7

29

Letter Mission

Name _____

Letter Writing Game

t

c

f

p

m

Name _____

Writer's Warm-Up

S S

S S

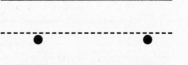

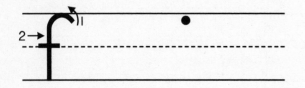

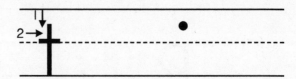

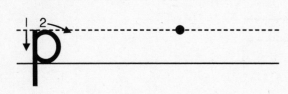

Activity 5

Writer's Warm-Up

S   S

S   S   •   • | •   •

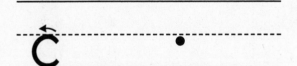

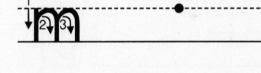

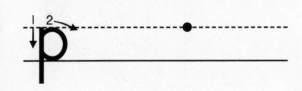

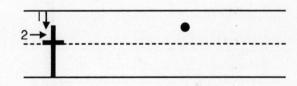

s t c f m

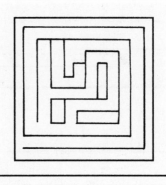

_____

- - - - - • - - - - -

_____

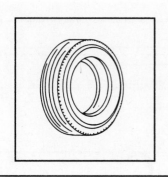

_____

- - - - - • - - - - -

_____

_____

- - - - - • - - - - -

_____

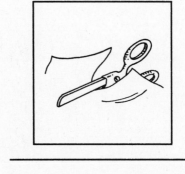

_____

- - - - - • - - - - -

_____

_____

- - - - - • - - - - -

_____

Writer's Warm-Up

d   d

d   d   •   •   •   •

f   •   s   •

p   •   t   •

m   •

c   •

Letter Cross-Out

Writer's Warm-Up

d   d

d   d   •   • | •   •

f   •   s   •

p   •   t   •

m   •

c   •

Name _____

Letter Race

d

s

t

c

Finish Line

© Pearson Education, Inc.

Letter Mission

Name _____

Letter Tag

→ d
   s
   t

→ c
   f
   m

→ m
   s
   c

→ t
   m
   d

→ f
   c
   s

→ m
   d
   t

Activity 7

40

Name _____

Writer's Warm-Up

f   s

p   t

d   m

c

© Pearson Education, Inc.

Activity 5

41

Letter Writing Game

t

p

c

d

m

s

Writer's Warm-Up

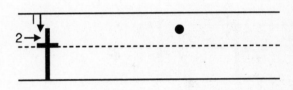

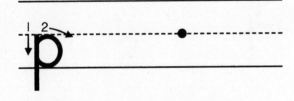

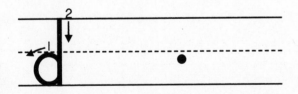

Writer's Warm-Up

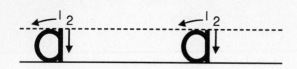

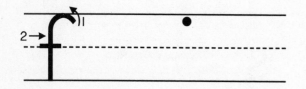

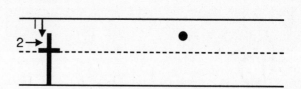

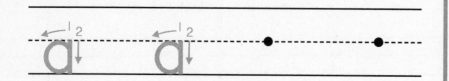

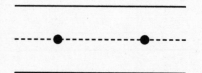

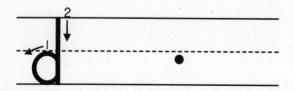

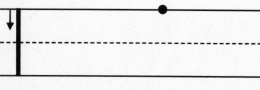

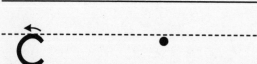

Name _____

First Sounds

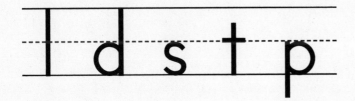

_____
• - - - - - - - - - - - -
_____

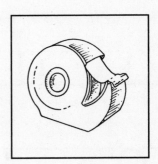

_____
• - - - - - - - - - - - -
_____

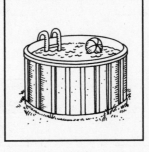

_____
- - - - - - • - - - - - -
_____

_____
- - - - - - • - - - - - -
_____

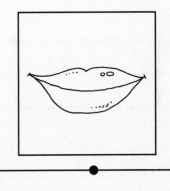

_____•_____
- - - - - - - - - - - -
_____

Activity 7

Writer's Warm-Up

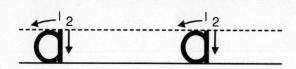

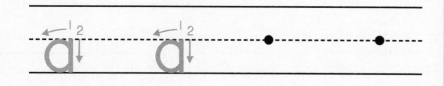 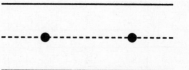

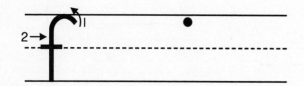 

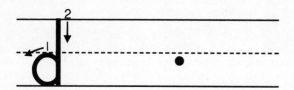 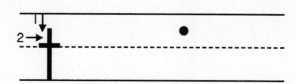

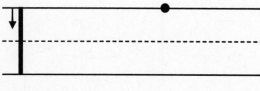

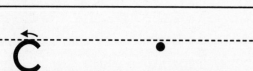

Activity 5
46

Letter Cross-Out

d   l   s

c   a   a

l   s   d

c

Letter Mission

Letter Race

l

a

s

d

Finish Line

Finish Line

Finish Line

Finish Line

Name _____

Writer's Warm-Up

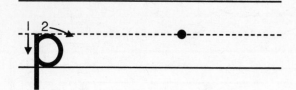

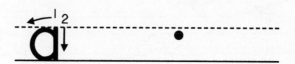

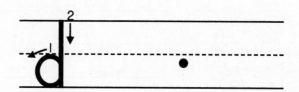

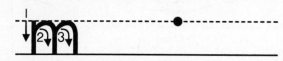

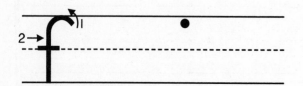

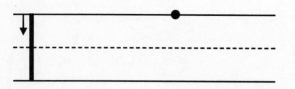

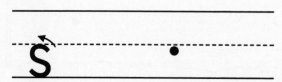

Letter Tag

→ a
l
d

→ s
f
m

→ m
a
l

→ d
s
a

→ s
d
m

→ f
a
l

Letter Writing Game

l

S

c

a

t

d

Name _____

Letter Mission

Name _____

Writer's Warm-Up

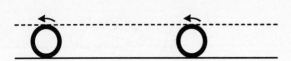

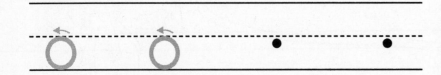

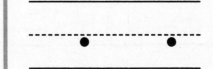

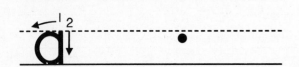

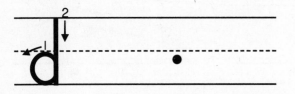

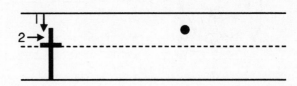

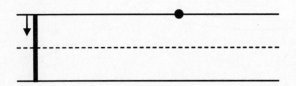

Letter Cross-Out

Activity 7

55

Writer's Warm-Up

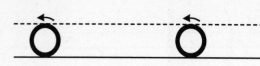

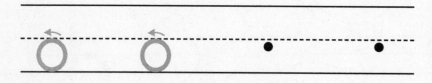

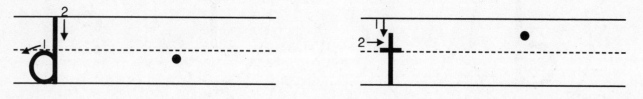

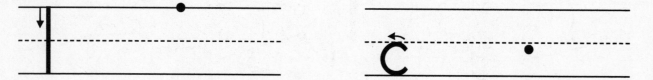

Tic-Tac-Toe

p	l	f
s	t	c
m	d	s

f	s	d
l	c	t
t	p	a

c	t	m
p	l	s
t	f	d

Letter Race

Finish Line

l

Finish Line

d

Finish Line

t

Finish Line

p

Name _____

Writer's Warm-Up

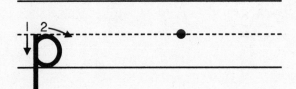

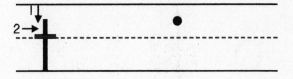

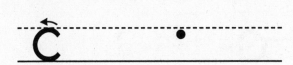

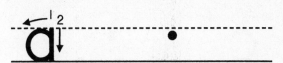

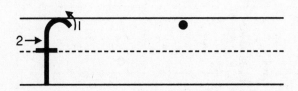

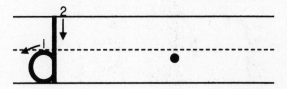

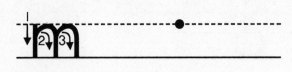

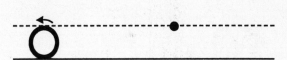

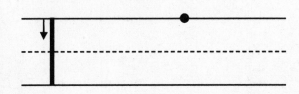

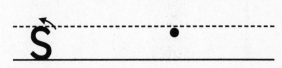

Name _____

Writer's Warm-Up

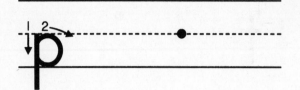

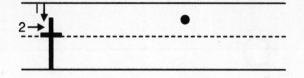

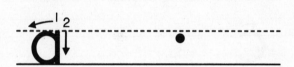

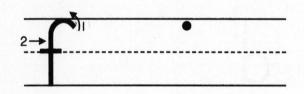

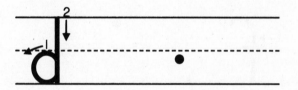

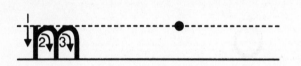

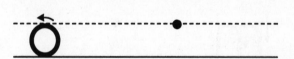

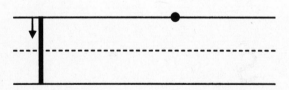

Activity 5

60

Tic-Tac-Toe

p	l	f
s	t	c
m	d	s

f	s	d
l	c	t
t	p	a

c	t	m
p	l	s
t	f	d

Letter Mission

© Pearson Education, Inc.

Name _____

Letter Writing Game

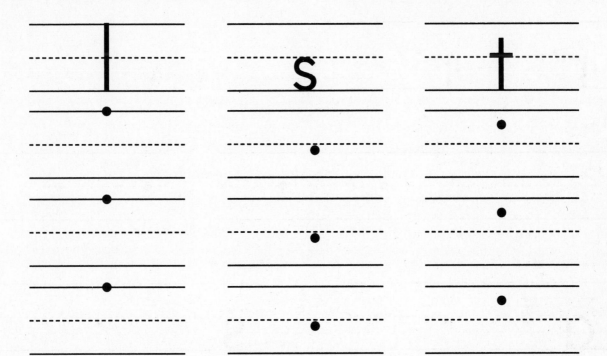

Writer's Warm-Up

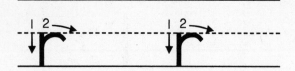

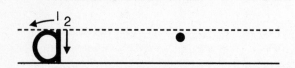

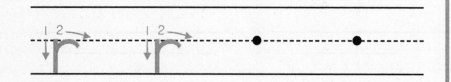

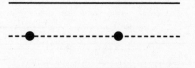

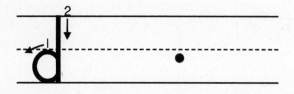

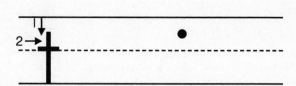

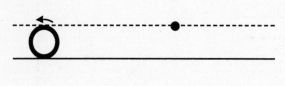

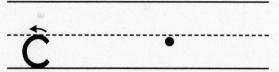

First and Last Sounds

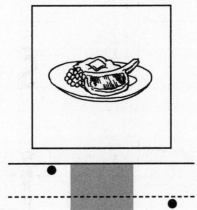

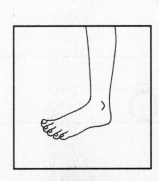

Writer's Warm-Up

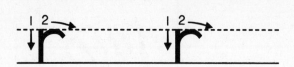

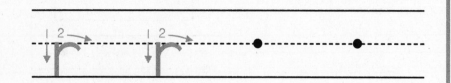

 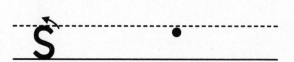

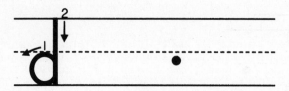 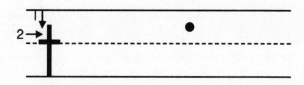

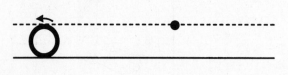 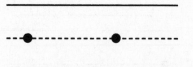

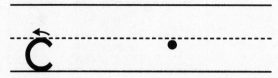

Name _____

Tic-Tac-Toe

1

p		s
l		p
m		m

4

s		t
f		l
d		m

2

l		p
c		t
t		d

5

d		t
c		l
s		p

3

m		t
s		l
f		s

6

c		p
t		l
m		f

Activity 7

67

Word Writing Game

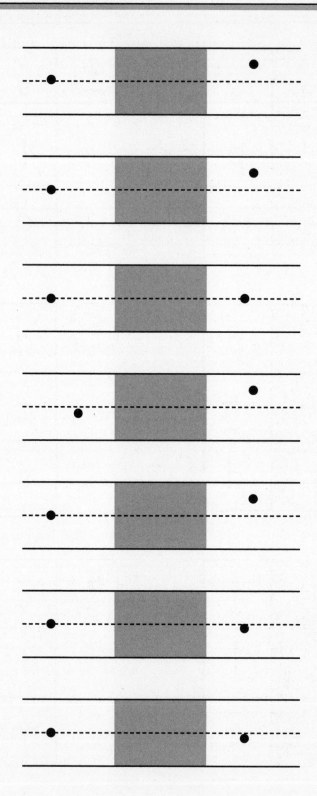

Name _____

Writer's Warm-Up

p

t

c

a

f

d

m

o

r

s

l

Activity 5

Word Maze

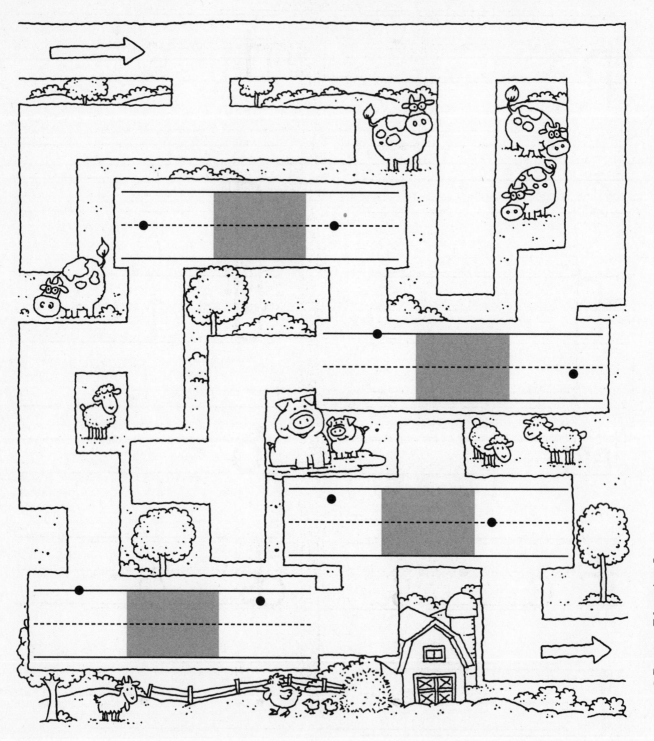

Activity 7

Writer's Warm-Up

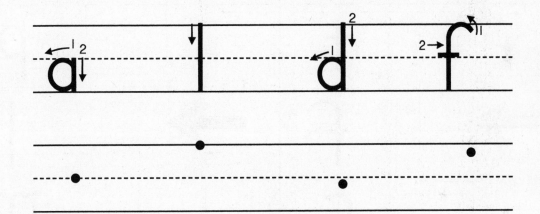

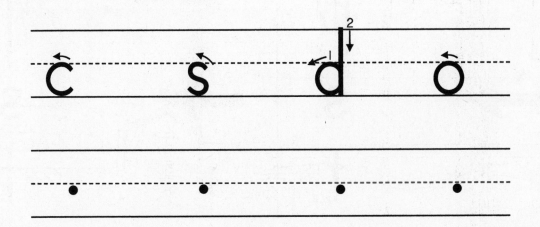

Letter Tag

→ l
   m
   p

→ s
   t
   f

→ t
   f
   c

→ p
   l
   m

→ p
   s
   t

→ l
   s
   t

Treasure Hunt

73

Rhyme Time

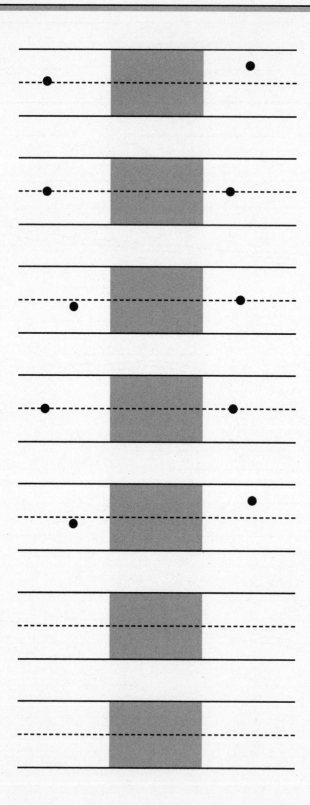